D0778965

IF FOUND,
please return to:

NAME: _____

ADDRESS: _____

_____

PHONE NUMBER: _____

E-MAIL: _____

MY one LINE A DAY

A THREE-YEAR MEMORY BOOK

chronicle books · san francisco

Copyright © 2013 by Chronicle Books LLC.
All rights reserved. No part of this product may be reproduced
in any form without written permission from the publisher.

ISBN 978-1-4521-1286-2

Design and illustrations by **LAUREN MICHELLE SMITH**.

Manufactured in China.

10 9 8 7 6 5 4 3 2

See the full range of **ONE LINE A DAY**
products at www.chroniclebooks.com.

CHRONICLE BOOKS LLC
680 Second Street
San Francisco, CA 94107

www.chroniclekids.com

A CONDENSED, COMPARATIVE RECORD FOR DOCUMENTING
LIFE'S BEST MOMENTS OVER THE COURSE OF THREE YEARS.

HOW TO USE THIS BOOK

To begin, turn to today's calendar date and fill in
the year for the first entry on the page. Here, you
can add your thoughts on the present day's events.
Tomorrow, repeat those steps, and continue to do so
for the rest of the year. When you've completed a full
year of entries, start the next year in the second entry
space on the page. And start the third year in the
third entry space on the page. Then, compare year-
by-year for all kinds of interesting discoveries!

JANUARY 1

20____ _____

_____

_____

_____

20____ _____

_____

_____

_____

20____ _____

_____

_____

_____

JANUARY 2

20 ___ _____

_____

_____

_____

20 ___ _____

_____

_____

_____

20 ___ _____

_____

_____

_____

JANUARY 3

20 ___ _____

_____

_____

_____

20 ___ _____

_____

_____

_____

20 ___ _____

_____

_____

_____

JANUARY 4

20 _____

20 _____

20 _____

JANUARY 5

20 _____

20 _____

20 _____

JANUARY 6

20____ _____

_____

_____

_____

20____ _____

_____

_____

_____

20____ _____

_____

_____

_____

JANUARY 7

20 _____ _____

_____

_____

_____

20 _____ _____

_____

_____

_____

20 _____ _____

_____

_____

_____

JANUARY 8

20____ _____

_____

_____

_____

20____ _____

_____

_____

_____

20____ _____

_____

_____

_____

JANUARY 9

20 _____ _____

_____

_____

_____

20 _____ _____

_____

_____

_____

20 _____ _____

_____

_____

_____

JANUARY 10

20 _____

20 _____

20 _____

JANUARY 11

20 _____

20 _____

20 _____

JANUARY 12

20 _____ _____

_____

_____

_____

20 _____ _____

_____

_____

_____

20 _____ _____

_____

_____

_____

JANUARY 13

20____ _____

_____

_____

_____

20____ _____

_____

_____

_____

20____ _____

_____

_____

_____

JANUARY 14

20 ____ _____

_____

_____

_____

20 ____ _____

_____

_____

_____

20 ____ _____

_____

_____

_____

JANUARY 15

20 _____ _____

_____

_____

_____

20 _____ _____

_____

_____

_____

20 _____ _____

_____

_____

_____

JANUARY 16

20 _____

20 _____

20 _____

JANUARY 17

20 _____

20 _____

20 _____

JANUARY 18

20 _____ _____

_____

_____

_____

20 _____ _____

_____

_____

_____

20 _____ _____

_____

_____

_____

JANUARY 19

20 _____ _____

_____

_____

_____

20 _____ _____

_____

_____

_____

20 _____ _____

_____

_____

_____

JANUARY 20

20 _____ _____

_____

_____

_____

20 _____ _____

_____

_____

_____

20 _____ _____

_____

_____

_____

20 _____ _____

_____

_____

_____

20 _____ _____

_____

_____

_____

20 _____ _____

_____

_____

_____

JANUARY 22

20 _____

20 _____

20 _____

JANUARY 23

20 ____

20 ____

20 ____

JANUARY 24

20 _____ _____

_____

_____

_____

20 _____ _____

_____

_____

_____

20 _____ _____

_____

_____

_____

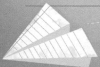

JANUARY 25

20 _____ _____
_____
_____
_____

20 _____ _____
_____
_____
_____

20 _____ _____
_____
_____
_____

JANUARY 26

20_____ _____

_____

_____

_____

20_____ _____

_____

_____

_____

20_____ _____

_____

_____

_____

JANUARY 27

20 _____ _____

_____

_____

_____

20 _____ _____

_____

_____

_____

20 _____ _____

_____

_____

_____

JANUARY 28

20 _____

20 _____

20 _____

JANUARY 29

20 ___

20 ___

20 ___

JANUARY 30

20_____ _____

_____

_____

_____

20_____ _____

_____

_____

_____

20_____ _____

_____

_____

_____

JANUARY 31

20 _____ _____

_____

_____

_____

20 _____ _____

_____

_____

_____

20 _____ _____

_____

_____

_____

FEBRUARY 1

20____ _____

_____

_____

_____

20____ _____

_____

_____

_____

20____ _____

_____

_____

_____

FEBRUARY 2

20____ _____

_____

_____

_____

20____ _____

_____

_____

_____

20____ _____

_____

_____

_____

FEBRUARY 3

20 ____

20 ____

20 ____

FEBRUARY 4

20 _____

20 _____

20 _____

FEBRUARY 5

20 _____ _____

_____

_____

_____

20 _____ _____

_____

_____

_____

20 _____ _____

_____

_____

_____

FEBRUARY 6

20____ _____

_____

_____

_____

20____ _____

_____

_____

_____

20____ _____

_____

_____

_____

FEBRUARY 7

20____ _____

_____

_____

_____

20____ _____

_____

_____

_____

20____ _____

_____

_____

_____

FEBRUARY 8

20 _____ _____

_____

_____

_____

20 _____ _____

_____

_____

_____

20 _____ _____

_____

_____

_____

FEBRUARY 9

20 _____

20 _____

20 _____

20 _____

20 _____

20 _____

FEBRUARY 11

20 ___ _____

_____

_____

_____

20 ___ _____

_____

_____

_____

20 ___ _____

_____

_____

_____

FEBRUARY 12

20 _____ _____

_____

_____

_____

20 _____ _____

_____

_____

_____

20 _____ _____

_____

_____

_____

FEBRUARY 13

20 _____ _____

_____

_____

_____

20 _____ _____

_____

_____

_____

20 _____ _____

_____

_____

_____

FEBRUARY 14

20 _____ _____

_____

_____

_____

20 _____ _____

_____

_____

_____

20 _____ _____

_____

_____

_____

FEBRUARY 15

20____

20____

20____

FEBRUARY 16

20 _____

20 _____

20 _____

FEBRUARY 17

20 _____ _____

_____

_____

_____

20 _____ _____

_____

_____

_____

20 _____ _____

_____

_____

_____

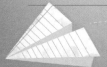

FEBRUARY 18

20____ _____

_____

_____

_____

20____ _____

_____

_____

_____

20____ _____

_____

_____

_____

FEBRUARY 19

20 _____ _____

_____

_____

_____

20 _____ _____

_____

_____

_____

20 _____ _____

_____

_____

_____

FEBRUARY 20

20 _____ _____

_____

_____

_____

20 _____ _____

_____

_____

_____

20 _____ _____

_____

_____

_____

FEBRUARY 21

20 _____

20 _____

20 _____

20 _____

20 _____

20 _____

FEBRUARY 23

20 _____ _____

_____

_____

_____

20 _____ _____

_____

_____

_____

20 _____ _____

_____

_____

_____

FEBRUARY 24

20 ___ _____

_____

_____

_____

20 ___ _____

_____

_____

_____

20 ___ _____

_____

_____

_____

FEBRUARY 25

20 _____ _____

_____

_____

_____

20 _____ _____

_____

_____

_____

20 _____ _____

_____

_____

_____

FEBRUARY 26

20 ___ _____

_____

_____

_____

20 ___ _____

_____

_____

_____

20 ___ _____

_____

_____

_____

FEBRUARY 27

20 _____

20 _____

20 _____

FEBRUARY 28

20 ___

20 ___

20 ___

FEBRUARY 29

20____ _____

_____

_____

_____

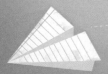

MARCH 1

20___ _____

_____

_____

_____

20___ _____

_____

_____

_____

20___ _____

_____

_____

_____

MARCH 2

20____ _____

_____

_____

_____

20____ _____

_____

_____

_____

20____ _____

_____

_____

_____

MARCH 3

20 ___ _____

_____

_____

_____

20 ___ _____

_____

_____

_____

20 ___ _____

_____

_____

_____

MARCH 4

20 _____

20 _____

20 _____

MARCH 5

20 ____

20 ____

20 ____

MARCH 6

20 _____ _____

_____

_____

_____

20 _____ _____

_____

_____

_____

20 _____ _____

_____

_____

_____

MARCH 7

20 _____ _____

_____

_____

_____

20 _____ _____

_____

_____

_____

20 _____ _____

_____

_____

_____

MARCH 8

20 _____ _____

_____

_____

_____

20 _____ _____

_____

_____

_____

20 _____ _____

_____

_____

_____

20 _____ _____

_____

_____

_____

20 _____ _____

_____

_____

_____

20 _____ _____

_____

_____

_____

MARCH 10

20 _____

20 _____

20 _____

MARCH 11

20 _____

20 _____

20 _____

MARCH 12

20 _____ _____
_____
_____
_____

20 _____ _____
_____
_____
_____

20 _____ _____
_____
_____
_____

MARCH 13

20 _____ _____

_____

_____

_____

20 _____ _____

_____

_____

_____

20 _____ _____

_____

_____

_____

MARCH 14

20 _____ _____

_____

_____

_____

20 _____ _____

_____

_____

_____

20 _____ _____

_____

_____

_____

MARCH 15

20____ _____

_____

_____

_____

20____ _____

_____

_____

_____

20____ _____

_____

_____

_____

MARCH 16

20 _____

20 _____

20 _____

MARCH 17

20 _____

20 _____

20 _____

MARCH 18

20 _____ _____

_____

_____

_____

20 _____ _____

_____

_____

_____

20 _____ _____

_____

_____

_____

MARCH 19

20 _____ _____

_____

_____

_____

20 _____ _____

_____

_____

_____

20 _____ _____

_____

_____

_____

MARCH 20

20 _____ _____

_____

_____

_____

20 _____ _____

_____

_____

_____

20 _____ _____

_____

_____

_____

MARCH 21

20 _____ _____

_____

_____

_____

20 _____ _____

_____

_____

_____

20 _____ _____

_____

_____

_____

MARCH 22

20 ___

20 ___

20 ___

MARCH 23

20 ___

20 ___

20 ___

MARCH 24

20 _____ _____

_____

_____

_____

20 _____ _____

_____

_____

_____

20 _____ _____

_____

_____

_____

MARCH 25

20 _____ _____

_____

_____

_____

20 _____ _____

_____

_____

_____

20 _____ _____

_____

_____

_____

MARCH 26

20 _____ _____

_____

_____

_____

20 _____ _____

_____

_____

_____

20 _____ _____

_____

_____

_____

MARCH 27

20 _____ _____

_____

_____

_____

20 _____ _____

_____

_____

_____

20 _____ _____

_____

_____

_____

MARCH 28

20 _____

20 _____

20 _____

20 _____

20 _____

20 _____

MARCH 30

20 _____ _____

_____

_____

_____

20 _____ _____

_____

_____

_____

20 _____ _____

_____

_____

_____

MARCH 31

20 _____ _____

_____

_____

_____

20 _____ _____

_____

_____

_____

20 _____ _____

_____

_____

_____

APRIL 1

20 _____ _____

_____

_____

_____

20 _____ _____

_____

_____

_____

20 _____ _____

_____

_____

_____

20 _____ _____

_____

_____

_____

20 _____ _____

_____

_____

_____

20 _____ _____

_____

_____

_____

APRIL 3

20 ___

20 ___

20 ___

APRIL 4

20 _____

20 _____

20 _____

APRIL 5

20 _____ _____

_____

_____

_____

_____

20 _____ _____

_____

_____

_____

20 _____ _____

_____

_____

_____

APRIL 6

20 _____ _____

_____

_____

_____

20 _____ _____

_____

_____

_____

20 _____ _____

_____

_____

_____

APRIL 7

20 _____ _____

_____

_____

_____

20 _____ _____

_____

_____

_____

20 _____ _____

_____

_____

_____

APRIL 8

20 ___ _____

_____

_____

_____

20 ___ _____

_____

_____

_____

20 ___ _____

_____

_____

_____

APRIL 9

20 _____

20 _____

20 _____

20 _____

20 _____

20 _____

APRIL 11

20 ___ _____

_____

_____

_____

20 ___ _____

_____

_____

_____

20 ___ _____

_____

_____

_____

APRIL 12

20 _____ _____

_____

_____

_____

20 _____ _____

_____

_____

_____

20 _____ _____

_____

_____

_____

APRIL 13

20 ___ _____

_____

_____

_____

20 ___ _____

_____

_____

_____

20 ___ _____

_____

_____

_____

APRIL 14

20 _____ _____

_____

_____

_____

20 _____ _____

_____

_____

_____

20 _____ _____

_____

_____

_____

APRIL 15

20 _____

20 _____

20 _____

APRIL 16

20 _____

20 _____

20 _____

APRIL 17

20 _____ _____

_____

_____

_____

20 _____ _____

_____

_____

_____

20 _____ _____

_____

_____

_____

APRIL 18

20 _____ _____

_____

_____

_____

20 _____ _____

_____

_____

_____

20 _____ _____

_____

_____

_____

APRIL 19

20 _____ _____

_____

_____

_____

20 _____ _____

_____

_____

_____

20 _____ _____

_____

_____

_____

APRIL 20

20 ____ _____

_____

_____

_____

20 ____ _____

_____

_____

_____

20 ____ _____

_____

_____

_____

APRIL 21

20 _____

20 _____

20 _____

20 _____

20 _____

20 _____

APRIL 23

20 ___ _____

_____

_____

_____

20 ___ _____

_____

_____

_____

20 ___ _____

_____

_____

_____

APRIL 24

20____ _____

_____

_____

_____

20____ _____

_____

_____

_____

20____ _____

_____

_____

_____

APRIL 25

20 _____ _____

_____

_____

_____

20 _____ _____

_____

_____

_____

20 _____ _____

_____

_____

_____

APRIL 26

20 _____ _____

_____

_____

_____

20 _____ _____

_____

_____

_____

20 _____ _____

_____

_____

_____

APRIL 27

20 _____

20 _____

20 _____

APRIL 28

20 _____

20 _____

20 _____

APRIL 29

20 _____ _____

_____

_____

_____

20 _____ _____

_____

_____

_____

20 _____ _____

_____

_____

_____

APRIL 30

20 ___ _____
_____
_____
_____

20 ___ _____
_____
_____
_____

20 ___ _____
_____
_____
_____

MAY 1

20 _____ _____

_____

_____

_____

20 _____ _____

_____

_____

_____

20 _____ _____

_____

_____

_____

MAY 2

20 _____ _____

_____

_____

_____

20 _____ _____

_____

_____

_____

20 _____ _____

_____

_____

_____

20 _____

20 _____

20 _____

20 _____

20 _____

20 _____

MAY 5

20___ _____

_____

_____

_____

20___ _____

_____

_____

_____

20___ _____

_____

_____

_____

MAY 6

20 _____ _____

_____

_____

_____

20 _____ _____

_____

_____

_____

20 _____ _____

_____

_____

_____

MAY 7

20 ___ _____

_____

_____

_____

20 ___ _____

_____

_____

_____

20 ___ _____

_____

_____

_____

MAY 8

20 _____ _____

_____

_____

_____

20 _____ _____

_____

_____

_____

20 _____ _____

_____

_____

_____

MAY 9

20 ___

20 ___

20 ___

MAY 10

20 _____

20 _____

20 _____

MAY 11

20____ _____

_____

_____

_____

20____ _____

_____

_____

_____

20____ _____

_____

_____

_____

MAY 12

20___ _____

_____

_____

_____

20___ _____

_____

_____

_____

20___ _____

_____

_____

_____

MAY 13

20 _____ _____

_____

_____

_____

20 _____ _____

_____

_____

_____

20 _____ _____

_____

_____

_____

MAY 14

20 _____ _____

_____

_____

_____

20 _____ _____

_____

_____

_____

20 _____ _____

_____

_____

_____

20 _____

20 _____

20 _____

20 _____

20 _____

20 _____

MAY 17

20 _____ _____

_____

_____

_____

20 _____ _____

_____

_____

_____

20 _____ _____

_____

_____

_____

MAY 18

20 _____ _____

_____

_____

_____

20 _____ _____

_____

_____

_____

20 _____ _____

_____

_____

_____

MAY 19

20 _____ _____

_____

_____

_____

20 _____ _____

_____

_____

_____

20 _____ _____

_____

_____

_____

MAY 20

20 _____ _____

_____

_____

_____

20 _____ _____

_____

_____

_____

20 _____ _____

_____

_____

_____

MAY 21

20 _____

20 _____

20 _____

MAY 22

20 ___

20 ___

20 ___

MAY 23

20___ _____

_____

_____

_____

20___ _____

_____

_____

_____

20___ _____

_____

_____

_____

MAY 24

20 _____ _____

_____

_____

_____

20 _____ _____

_____

_____

_____

20 _____ _____

_____

_____

_____

MAY 25

20 _____ _____

_____

_____

_____

20 _____ _____

_____

_____

_____

20 _____ _____

_____

_____

_____

MAY 26

20 _____ _____

_____

_____

_____

20 _____ _____

_____

_____

_____

20 _____ _____

_____

_____

_____

MAY 27

20 _____

20 _____

20 _____

MAY 28

20 ___

20 ___

20 ___

MAY 29

20 _____ _____

_____

_____

_____

20 _____ _____

_____

_____

_____

20 _____ _____

_____

_____

_____

MAY 30

20 _____ _____

_____

_____

_____

20 _____ _____

_____

_____

_____

20 _____ _____

_____

_____

_____

MAY 31

20 ___ _____

_____

_____

_____

20 ___ _____

_____

_____

_____

20 ___ _____

_____

_____

_____

JUNE 1

20 _____ _____

_____

_____

_____

20 _____ _____

_____

_____

_____

20 _____ _____

_____

_____

_____

JUNE 2

20 _____

20 _____

20 _____

JUNE 3

20 ___

20 ___

20 ___

JUNE 4

20 _____ _____

_____

_____

_____

20 _____ _____

_____

_____

_____

20 _____ _____

_____

_____

_____

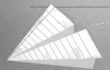

JUNE 5

20 _____ _____
_____
_____
_____

20 _____ _____
_____
_____
_____

20 _____ _____
_____
_____
_____

JUNE 6

20 _____ _____

_____

_____

_____

20 _____ _____

_____

_____

_____

20 _____ _____

_____

_____

_____

JUNE 7

20 _____ _____

_____

_____

_____

20 _____ _____

_____

_____

_____

20 _____ _____

_____

_____

_____

JUNE 8

20 _____

20 _____

20 _____

JUNE 9

20 ___

20 ___

20 ___

JUNE 10

20 _____ _____

_____

_____

_____

20 _____ _____

_____

_____

_____

20 _____ _____

_____

_____

_____

JUNE 11

20 _____ _____

_____

_____

_____

20 _____ _____

_____

_____

_____

20 _____ _____

_____

_____

_____

JUNE 12

20 _____ _____

_____

_____

_____

_____

20 _____ _____

_____

_____

_____

20 _____ _____

_____

_____

_____

JUNE 13

20 ___ _____

_____

_____

_____

20 ___ _____

_____

_____

_____

20 ___ _____

_____

_____

_____

JUNE 14

20 ___

20 ___

20 ___

JUNE 15

20 _____

20 _____

20 _____

JUNE 16

20 _____ _____

_____

_____

_____

20 _____ _____

_____

_____

_____

20 _____ _____

_____

_____

_____

JUNE 17

20 _____ _____

_____

_____

_____

20 _____ _____

_____

_____

_____

20 _____ _____

_____

_____

_____

JUNE 18

20 _____ _____

_____

_____

_____

20 _____ _____

_____

_____

_____

20 _____ _____

_____

_____

_____

JUNE 19

20 _____ _____

_____

_____

_____

20 _____ _____

_____

_____

_____

20 _____ _____

_____

_____

_____

20 _____

20 _____

20 _____

JUNE 21

20 _____

20 _____

20 _____

JUNE 22

20 ___ _____

_____

_____

_____

20 ___ _____

_____

_____

_____

20 ___ _____

_____

_____

_____

JUNE 23

20 ___ _____

_____

_____

_____

20 ___ _____

_____

_____

_____

20 ___ _____

_____

_____

_____

JUNE 24

20 _____ _____

_____

_____

_____

20 _____ _____

_____

_____

_____

20 _____ _____

_____

_____

_____

20 _____ _____

_____

_____

_____

20 _____ _____

_____

_____

_____

20 _____ _____

_____

_____

_____

JUNE 26

20 _____

20 _____

20 _____

JUNE 27

20 _____

20 _____

20 _____

JUNE 28

20____ _____

_____

_____

_____

20____ _____

_____

_____

_____

20____ _____

_____

_____

_____

JUNE 29

20 _____ _____

_____

_____

_____

20 _____ _____

_____

_____

_____

20 _____ _____

_____

_____

_____

JUNE 30

20 _____ _____

_____

_____

_____

20 _____ _____

_____

_____

_____

20 _____ _____

_____

_____

_____

JULY 1

20 ___ _____

_____

_____

_____

20 ___ _____

_____

_____

_____

20 ___ _____

_____

_____

_____

JULY 2

20 _____

20 _____

20 _____

20 ____

20 ____

20 ____

JULY 4

20 ___ _____

_____

_____

_____

20 ___ _____

_____

_____

_____

20 ___ _____

_____

_____

_____

JULY 5

20 _____ _____

_____

_____

_____

20 _____ _____

_____

_____

_____

20 _____ _____

_____

_____

_____

JULY 6

20 _____ _____

_____

_____

_____

20 _____ _____

_____

_____

_____

20 _____ _____

_____

_____

_____

JULY 7

20 _____ _____

_____

_____

_____

20 _____ _____

_____

_____

_____

20 _____ _____

_____

_____

_____

JULY 8

20 _____

20 _____

20 _____

JULY 9

20 _____

20 _____

20 _____

JULY 10

20 ___ _____

_____

_____

_____

20 ___ _____

_____

_____

_____

20 ___ _____

_____

_____

_____

JULY 11

20 _____ _____

_____

_____

_____

20 _____ _____

_____

_____

_____

20 _____ _____

_____

_____

_____

JULY 12

20 _____ _____

_____

_____

_____

20 _____ _____

_____

_____

_____

20 _____ _____

_____

_____

_____

JULY 13

20 _____ _____

_____

_____

_____

20 _____ _____

_____

_____

_____

20 _____ _____

_____

_____

_____

20 _____

20 _____

20 _____

JULY 15

20 _____

20 _____

20 _____

JULY 16

20 _____ _____

_____

_____

_____

20 _____ _____

_____

_____

_____

20 _____ _____

_____

_____

_____

JULY 17

20 ____ _____

_____

_____

_____

20 ____ _____

_____

_____

_____

20 ____ _____

_____

_____

_____

JULY 18

20 _____ _____

_____

_____

_____

20 _____ _____

_____

_____

_____

20 _____ _____

_____

_____

_____

JULY 19

20 _____ _____

_____

_____

_____

20 _____ _____

_____

_____

_____

20 _____ _____

_____

_____

_____

JULY 20

20 _____

20 _____

20 _____

JULY 21

20 _____

20 _____

20 _____

JULY 22

20 ___ _____

_____

_____

_____

20 ___ _____

_____

_____

_____

20 ___ _____

_____

_____

JULY 23

20 _____ _____

_____

_____

_____

20 _____ _____

_____

_____

_____

20 _____ _____

_____

_____

_____

JULY 24

20 _____ _____

_____

_____

_____

20 _____ _____

_____

_____

_____

20 _____ _____

_____

_____

_____

JULY 25

20 _____ _____

_____

_____

_____

20 _____ _____

_____

_____

_____

20 _____ _____

_____

_____

_____

20 _____

20 _____

20 _____

JULY 27

20 _____

20 _____

20 _____

JULY 28

20 ___ _____

_____

_____

_____

20 ___ _____

_____

_____

_____

20 ___ _____

_____

_____

_____

JULY 29

20 _____ _____

_____

_____

_____

20 _____ _____

_____

_____

_____

20 _____ _____

_____

_____

_____

JULY 30

20 _____ _____

_____

_____

_____

20 _____ _____

_____

_____

_____

20 _____ _____

_____

_____

_____

JULY 31

20 ___ _____

_____

_____

_____

20 ___ _____

_____

_____

_____

20 ___ _____

_____

_____

_____

AUGUST 1

20 _____

20 _____

20 _____

AUGUST 2

20 ___

20 ___

20 ___

AUGUST 3

20 _____ _____

_____

_____

_____

20 _____ _____

_____

_____

_____

20 _____ _____

_____

_____

AUGUST 4

20 _____ _____

_____

_____

_____

20 _____ _____

_____

_____

_____

20 _____ _____

_____

_____

_____

AUGUST 5

20 ___ _____

_____

_____

_____

20 ___ _____

_____

_____

_____

20 ___ _____

_____

_____

_____

AUGUST 6

20 _____ _____

_____

_____

_____

20 _____ _____

_____

_____

_____

20 _____ _____

_____

_____

_____

AUGUST 7

20 _____

20 _____

20 _____

20 ___

20 ___

20 ___

AUGUST 9

20 _____ _____

_____

_____

_____

20 _____ _____

_____

_____

20 _____ _____

_____

_____

_____

AUGUST 10

20 _____ _____

_____

_____

_____

20 _____ _____

_____

_____

_____

20 _____ _____

_____

_____

_____

AUGUST 11

20 _____ _____

_____

_____

_____

20 _____ _____

_____

_____

_____

20 _____ _____

_____

_____

_____

20 ___ _____

_____

_____

_____

20 ___ _____

_____

_____

_____

20 ___ _____

_____

_____

_____

AUGUST 13

20 ____

20 ____

20 ____

AUGUST 14

20 _____

20 _____

20 _____

AUGUST 15

20 _____ _____

_____

_____

_____

20 _____ _____

_____

_____

_____

20 _____ _____

_____

_____

_____

AUGUST 16

20 _____ _____

_____

_____

_____

20 _____ _____

_____

_____

_____

20 _____ _____

_____

_____

_____

AUGUST 17

20 ___ _____

_____

_____

_____

20 ___ _____

_____

_____

_____

20 ___ _____

_____

_____

_____

AUGUST 18

20 _____ _____

_____

_____

_____

20 _____ _____

_____

_____

_____

20 _____ _____

_____

_____

_____

20 _____

20 _____

20 _____

20 _____

20 _____

20 _____

AUGUST 21

20 _____ _____

_____

_____

_____

20 _____ _____

_____

_____

_____

20 _____ _____

_____

_____

_____

AUGUST 22

20 _____ _____

_____

_____

_____

20 _____ _____

_____

_____

_____

20 _____ _____

_____

_____

_____

AUGUST 23

20 _____ _____

_____

_____

_____

20 _____ _____

_____

_____

_____

20 _____ _____

_____

_____

_____

AUGUST 24

20 _____ _____

_____

_____

_____

20 _____ _____

_____

_____

_____

20 _____ _____

_____

_____

_____

AUGUST 25

20 _____

20 _____

20 _____

AUGUST 26

20 _____

20 _____

20 _____

AUGUST 27

20 _____ _____

_____

_____

_____

20 _____ _____

_____

_____

_____

20 _____ _____

_____

_____

_____

AUGUST 28

20 _____ _____

_____

_____

_____

20 _____ _____

_____

_____

_____

20 _____ _____

_____

_____

_____

AUGUST 29

20 ___ _____

_____

_____

_____

20 ___ _____

_____

_____

_____

20 ___ _____

_____

_____

_____

AUGUST 30

20 _____ _____

_____

_____

_____

20 _____ _____

_____

_____

_____

20 _____ _____

_____

_____

_____

AUGUST 31

20 _____

20 _____

20 _____

SEPTEMBER 1

20 _____

20 _____

20 _____

SEPTEMBER 2

20____ _____

_____

_____

_____

20____ _____

_____

_____

_____

20____ _____

_____

_____

_____

SEPTEMBER 3

20 ____ _____

_____

_____

_____

20 ____ _____

_____

_____

_____

20 ____ _____

_____

_____

_____

SEPTEMBER 4

20 ___ _____

_____

_____

_____

20 ___ _____

_____

_____

_____

20 ___ _____

_____

_____

_____

20 _____ _____

_____

_____

_____

20 _____ _____

_____

_____

_____

20 _____ _____

_____

_____

_____

SEPTEMBER 6

20 _____

20 _____

20 _____

SEPTEMBER 7

20 ____

20 ____

20 ____

SEPTEMBER 8

20 _____ _____

_____

_____

_____

20 _____ _____

_____

_____

_____

20 _____ _____

_____

_____

_____

SEPTEMBER 9

20 _____ _____
_____
_____
_____

20 _____ _____
_____
_____
_____

20 _____ _____
_____
_____
_____

SEPTEMBER 10

20___ _____

_____

_____

_____

20___ _____

_____

_____

_____

20___ _____

_____

_____

_____

SEPTEMBER 11

20 _____ _____

_____

_____

_____

20 _____ _____

_____

_____

_____

20 _____ _____

_____

_____

_____

SEPTEMBER 12

20 _____

20 _____

20 _____

SEPTEMBER 13

20 ___

20 ___

20 ___

SEPTEMBER 14

20 _____ _____

_____

_____

_____

20 _____ _____

_____

_____

_____

20 _____ _____

_____

_____

_____

SEPTEMBER 15

20 _____ _____

_____

_____

_____

20 _____ _____

_____

_____

_____

20 _____ _____

_____

_____

_____

SEPTEMBER 16

20 _____ _____

_____

_____

_____

_____

20 _____ _____

_____

_____

_____

20 _____ _____

_____

_____

_____

SEPTEMBER 17

20___ _____

_____

_____

_____

20___ _____

_____

_____

_____

20___ _____

_____

_____

_____

SEPTEMBER 18

20 _____

20 _____

20 _____

SEPTEMBER 19

20 _____

20 _____

20 _____

SEPTEMBER 20

20 _____ _____

_____

_____

_____

20 _____ _____

_____

_____

_____

20 _____ _____

_____

_____

_____

SEPTEMBER 21

20 _____ _____

_____

_____

_____

20 _____ _____

_____

_____

_____

20 _____ _____

_____

_____

_____

SEPTEMBER 22

20 _____ _____

_____

_____

_____

20 _____ _____

_____

_____

_____

20 _____ _____

_____

_____

_____

SEPTEMBER 23

20 _____ _____

_____

_____

_____

20 _____ _____

_____

_____

_____

20 _____ _____

_____

_____

_____

20 _____

20 _____

20 _____

20 _____

20 _____

20 _____

SEPTEMBER 26

20____ _____

_____

_____

_____

20____ _____

_____

_____

_____

20____ _____

_____

_____

_____

SEPTEMBER 27

20 _____ _____

_____

_____

_____

20 _____ _____

_____

_____

_____

20 _____ _____

_____

_____

_____

SEPTEMBER 28

20 _____ _____

_____

_____

_____

20 _____ _____

_____

_____

_____

20 _____ _____

_____

_____

_____

SEPTEMBER 29

20 ___ _____

_____

_____

_____

20 ___ _____

_____

_____

_____

20 ___ _____

_____

_____

_____

SEPTEMBER 30

20 _____

20 _____

20 _____

OCTOBER 1

20 ___

20 ___

20 ___

OCTOBER 2

20 ___ _____

_____

_____

_____

20 ___ _____

_____

_____

_____

20 ___ _____

_____

_____

_____

OCTOBER 3

20 _____ _____

_____

_____

_____

20 _____ _____

_____

_____

_____

20 _____ _____

_____

_____

_____

OCTOBER 4

20 _____ _____

_____

_____

_____

20 _____ _____

_____

_____

_____

20 _____ _____

_____

_____

_____

OCTOBER 5

20 _____ _____

_____

_____

_____

20 _____ _____

_____

_____

_____

20 _____ _____

_____

_____

_____

OCTOBER 6

20 _____

20 _____

20 _____

20 _____

20 _____

20 _____

OCTOBER 8

20 ___ _____

_____

_____

_____

20 ___ _____

_____

_____

_____

20 ___ _____

_____

_____

_____

OCTOBER 9

20 ___ _____

_____

_____

_____

20 ___ _____

_____

_____

_____

20 ___ _____

_____

_____

_____

OCTOBER 10

20___ _____

_____

_____

_____

20___ _____

_____

_____

_____

20___ _____

_____

_____

_____

OCTOBER 11

20 _____ _____

_____

_____

_____

20 _____ _____

_____

_____

_____

20 _____ _____

_____

_____

_____

OCTOBER 12

20 _____

20 _____

20 _____

OCTOBER 13

20 _____

20 _____

20 _____

OCTOBER 14

20 _____ _____

_____

_____

_____

20 _____ _____

_____

_____

_____

20 _____ _____

_____

_____

_____

OCTOBER 15

20 _____ _____

_____

_____

_____

20 _____ _____

_____

_____

_____

20 _____ _____

_____

_____

_____

OCTOBER 16

20 _____ _____

_____

_____

_____

20 _____ _____

_____

_____

_____

20 _____ _____

_____

_____

_____

OCTOBER 17

20 ___ _____

_____

_____

_____

20 ___ _____

_____

_____

_____

20 ___ _____

_____

_____

_____

OCTOBER 18

20 _____

20 _____

20 _____

OCTOBER 19

20 ___

20 ___

20 ___

OCTOBER 20

20 _____ _____

_____

_____

_____

20 _____ _____

_____

_____

_____

20 _____ _____

_____

_____

_____

OCTOBER 21

20 _____ _____

_____

_____

_____

20 _____ _____

_____

_____

_____

20 _____ _____

_____

_____

_____

OCTOBER 22

20 _____ _____

_____

_____

_____

20 _____ _____

_____

_____

_____

20 _____ _____

_____

_____

_____

OCTOBER 23

20 _____ _____

_____

_____

_____

20 _____ _____

_____

_____

_____

20 _____ _____

_____

_____

_____

OCTOBER 24

20 _____

20 _____

20 _____

OCTOBER 25

20 _____

20 _____

20 _____

OCTOBER 26

20 ____ _____

_____

_____

_____

20 ____ _____

_____

_____

_____

20 ____ _____

_____

_____

_____

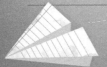

OCTOBER 27

20 _____ _____

_____

_____

_____

20 _____ _____

_____

_____

_____

20 _____ _____

_____

_____

_____

OCTOBER 28

20 _____ _____

_____

_____

_____

20 _____ _____

_____

_____

_____

20 _____ _____

_____

_____

_____

OCTOBER 29

20 ____ _____

_____

_____

_____

20 ____ _____

_____

_____

_____

20 ____ _____

_____

_____

_____

OCTOBER 30

20 _____

20 _____

20 _____

OCTOBER 31

20 ___

20 ___

20 ___

NOVEMBER 1

20 _____ _____

_____

_____

_____

20 _____ _____

_____

_____

_____

20 _____ _____

_____

_____

_____

NOVEMBER 2

20 ___ _____

_____

_____

_____

20 ___ _____

_____

_____

_____

20 ___ _____

_____

_____

_____

NOVEMBER 3

20 _____ _____

_____

_____

_____

20 _____ _____

_____

_____

_____

20 _____ _____

_____

_____

_____

NOVEMBER 4

20 ___ _____

_____

_____

_____

20 ___ _____

_____

_____

_____

20 ___ _____

_____

_____

_____

NOVEMBER 5

20 _____

20 _____

20 _____

NOVEMBER 6

20 _____

20 _____

20 _____

NOVEMBER 7

20 ___ _____

_____

_____

_____

20 ___ _____

_____

_____

_____

20 ___ _____

_____

_____

_____

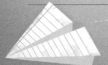

NOVEMBER 8

20 _____ _____

_____

_____

_____

20 _____ _____

_____

_____

_____

20 _____ _____

_____

_____

_____

NOVEMBER 9

20 _____ _____

_____

_____

_____

20 _____ _____

_____

_____

_____

20 _____ _____

_____

_____

_____

NOVEMBER 10

20 _____ _____

_____

_____

_____

20 _____ _____

_____

_____

_____

20 _____ _____

_____

_____

_____

NOVEMBER 11

20 _____

20 _____

20 _____

20 ____

20 ____

20 ____

NOVEMBER 13

20 _____ _____

_____

_____

_____

20 _____ _____

_____

_____

_____

20 _____ _____

_____

_____

_____

NOVEMBER 14

20 _____ _____

_____

_____

_____

20 _____ _____

_____

_____

_____

20 _____ _____

_____

_____

_____

NOVEMBER 15

20 _____ _____

_____

_____

_____

20 _____ _____

_____

_____

_____

20 _____ _____

_____

_____

_____

NOVEMBER 16

20 _____ _____

_____

_____

_____

20 _____ _____

_____

_____

_____

20 _____ _____

_____

_____

_____

NOVEMBER 17

20 _____

20 _____

20 _____

NOVEMBER 18

20 _____

20 _____

20 _____

NOVEMBER 19

20 _____ _____

_____

_____

_____

20 _____ _____

_____

_____

_____

20 _____ _____

_____

_____

NOVEMBER 20

20 _____ _____

_____

_____

_____

20 _____ _____

_____

_____

_____

20 _____ _____

_____

_____

_____

NOVEMBER 21

20___ _____

_____

_____

_____

20___ _____

_____

_____

_____

20___ _____

_____

_____

_____

NOVEMBER 22

20 _____ _____

_____

_____

_____

20 _____ _____

_____

_____

_____

20 _____ _____

_____

_____

_____

NOVEMBER 23

20 _____

20 _____

20 _____

NOVEMBER 24

20 ___

20 ___

20 ___

NOVEMBER 25

20 _____ _____

_____

_____

_____

20 _____ _____

_____

_____

_____

20 _____ _____

_____

_____

_____

NOVEMBER 26

20 _____ _____

_____

_____

_____

20 _____ _____

_____

_____

_____

20 _____ _____

_____

_____

_____

NOVEMBER 27

20 _____ _____

_____

_____

_____

20 _____ _____

_____

_____

_____

20 _____ _____

_____

_____

_____

NOVEMBER 28

20 _____ _____

_____

_____

_____

20 _____ _____

_____

_____

_____

20 _____ _____

_____

_____

_____

NOVEMBER 29

20 ____

20 ____

20 ____

NOVEMBER 30

20 _____

20 _____

20 _____

DECEMBER 1

20____ _____

_____

_____

_____

20____ _____

_____

_____

_____

20____ _____

_____

_____

_____

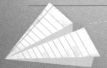

DECEMBER 2

20 ___ _____

_____

_____

_____

20 ___ _____

_____

_____

_____

20 ___ _____

_____

_____

_____

DECEMBER 3

20 _____ _____

_____

_____

_____

20 _____ _____ .

_____

_____

_____

20 _____ _____

_____

_____

_____

DECEMBER 4

20 _____ _____

_____

_____

_____

20 _____ _____

_____

_____

_____

20 _____ _____

_____

_____

_____

DECEMBER 5

20 _____

20 _____

20 _____

DECEMBER 6

20 ____

20 ____

20 ____

DECEMBER 7

20 ___ _____

_____

_____

_____

20 ___ _____

_____

_____

_____

20 ___ _____

_____

_____

_____

DECEMBER 8

20 ___ _____

_____

_____

_____

20 ___ _____

_____

_____

_____

20 ___ _____

_____

_____

_____

DECEMBER 9

20 _____ _____

_____

_____

_____

20 _____ _____

_____

_____

_____

20 _____ _____

_____

_____

_____

DECEMBER 10

20 ___ _____

_____

_____

_____

20 ___ _____

_____

_____

_____

20 ___ _____

_____

_____

_____

DECEMBER 11

20 _____

20 _____

20 _____

DECEMBER 12

20 _____

20 _____

20 _____

DECEMBER 13

20 _____ _____

_____

_____

_____

20 _____ _____

_____

_____

_____

20 _____ _____

_____

_____

_____

DECEMBER 14

20 _____ _____

_____

_____

_____

20 _____ _____

_____

_____

_____

20 _____ _____

_____

_____

_____

DECEMBER 15

20 _____ _____

_____

_____

_____

20 _____ _____

_____

_____

_____

20 _____ _____

_____

_____

_____

DECEMBER 16

20 _____ _____

_____

_____

_____

20 _____ _____

_____

_____

_____

20 _____ _____

_____

_____

_____

DECEMBER 17

20 _____

20 _____

20 _____

20 _____

20 _____

20 _____

DECEMBER 19

20 _____ _____

_____

_____

_____

20 _____ _____

_____

_____

_____

20 _____ _____

_____

_____

_____

DECEMBER 20

20 ___ _____

_____

_____

_____

20 ___ _____

_____

_____

_____

20 ___ _____

_____

_____

_____

DECEMBER 21

20 _____ _____

_____

_____

_____

20 _____ _____

_____

_____

_____

20 _____ _____

_____

_____

_____

DECEMBER 22

20 _____ _____

_____

_____

_____

20 _____ _____

_____

_____

_____

20 _____ _____

_____

_____

_____

DECEMBER 23

20 ___

20 ___

20 ___

DECEMBER 24

20 _____

20 _____

20 _____

DECEMBER 25

20 _____ _____

_____

_____

_____

20 _____ _____

_____

_____

_____

20 _____ _____

_____

_____

_____

DECEMBER 26

20 _____ _____

_____

_____

_____

20 _____ _____

_____

_____

_____

20 _____ _____

_____

_____

_____

DECEMBER 27

20 _____ _____

_____

_____

_____

20 _____ _____

_____

_____

_____

20 _____ _____

_____

_____

_____

DECEMBER 28

20 _____ _____

_____

_____

_____

20 _____ _____

_____

_____

_____

20 _____ _____

_____

_____

_____

DECEMBER 29

20 _____

20 _____

20 _____

DECEMBER 30

20 _____

20 _____

20 _____

DECEMBER 31

20 _____ _____

_____

_____

_____

20 _____ _____

_____

_____

_____

20 _____ _____

_____

_____

_____

dates to
REMEMBER

_____

_____

_____

_____

_____

_____

_____

_____

_____

_____

_____

dates to
REMEMBER